Hot Air Balloon

Jyotsna Krishnadev

BookLeaf Publishing

India | USA | UK

Presentation by *BookLeaf Publishing*

Web: www.bookleafpub.com

E-mail: info@bookleafpub.com

ISBN: 9789360941161

First edition 2024

For my maa,

Your unwavering support through every choice and decision I've made has been my greatest source of strength. You taught me to find the silver lining in every dark cloud, this learning has been pivotal in shaping my perspectives in life. Your wisdom and guidance taught me to find strength through all my ups and downs. Thank you for being my rock and my shield.

ACKNOWLEDGEMENT

My deepest gratitude and love to:
Divya: Thank you for believing in me and encouraging me to continue creating poems and continue writing. You lit the flame of poetry in me and inspired me to write my first poem at age 6! What a "Cart" that turned out to be!

Ishaan: His famous words "And then what happened?" inspired me to push through and work on the pile of unfinished poems I had lying around, collecting dust.

My mother (Sheila): For patiently pointing out when I was going overboard with "poetic licence". Thank you for being my in-house editor and reading through this collection.

PREFACE

Jyotsna Krishnadev is an Architect and a budding poet from Coonoor, The Nilgiris. She draws her inspiration from Nature and her experiences and learnings from everyday life.

Some of her narrative poetry along with her poems based on life's truths and teachings are compiled and published as an anecdotal collection of poems titled "Hot Air Balloon." She says "Reading poetry is like stepping into a hot air balloon and floating away on a journey into another realm."

Into the clouds we go

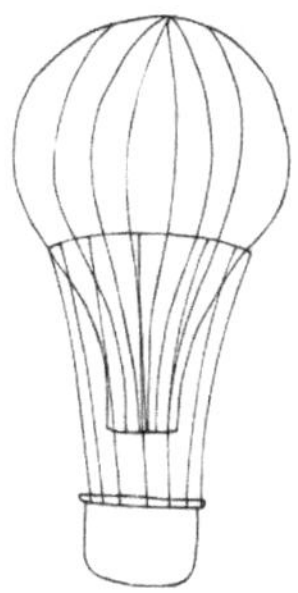

Beneath a sky that's blue and wide,
I pondered on a fanciful ride.
A hot air balloon, aloft and free,
To drift into realms unknown to me.

In a wicker basket, swaying light,
I contemplated; day turned to night.
To leave behind the mundane ground,
And seek the wonders yet unfound.

Above the world, where clouds convene,
A realm of dreams, serene, unseen.
Where whispers ride on Zephyrs' breath.
And lead to realms untouched by death.

A world where time is but a tease,
And every moment is at ease.
Amongst the clouds where shadows play,
A land of tea parties, night and day.

Where silver spoons and porcelain gleam,
And laughter dances in this dream.
With cakes of cloud and cups of mist,
In timeless joy, we all insist.

So let me rise, on wings of air,
To find that world beyond compare.
In a hot air balloon, I'll float on high,
And join the tea parties in the sky.

My first encounter

In the land where tea parties reign,
Day and night are much the same.
Amidst the clouds, where dreams take flight,
I stumbled upon a curious sight.

A talking phoenix, with feathers bright,
Perched upon a golden light.
With eyes that sparkled, wise and old,
His voice revealed tales never been told!

"Welcome, wanderer," he softly said,
As I gazed upon his fiery head.
"In this land of endless tea,
The secrets of the cards I'll reveal to thee."

With a tarot deck in taloned claw,
He beckoned me to take a draw.
Each card a story, ancient and deep,
Unfolding truths that I'd longed to keep.

Beneath the moon's enchanting glow,
We sipped our tea and watched it flow.
As the phoenix read the cards with care,
I found my destiny laid bare.

In this land where time stands still,
And dreams dance upon the sill,
The cards held visions, dark and bright
In this land of tea parties, day and night.

The reading

In a room aglow with twilight's embrace,
Where shadows linger, and time finds its space,
There sits a phoenix, with feathers aflame,
His eyes alight with an ancient flame.

With a flick of his wing, the cards take flight,
Each one a tale, in the realm of night.
The fool, he dances, with steps unsure,
Embarking on a journey, pure and true.

The magician conjures, with a sleight of hand,
Crafting dreams from shifting sand.
The high priestess whispers, secrets deep,
Destiny's dance, in an endless chase.

Death, a phoenix, rising from the pyre,
A transformation, in flames of fire.
The tower falls, with a thunderous sound,
Breaking illusions, on sacred ground.

The star, it twinkles, in the velvet sky,
A beacon of hope, for those who try.
And in the Moon's embrace, shadows dance,
Revealing truths, in a mystic trance.

The sun, it rises, in golden rays,
Dispelling darkness, in its warm embrace,
Judgement calls, with a solemn decree,
A reckoning come for you and me,

Finally, this world, in its own sphere,
A tapestry woven, of joy and fear.
And as the cards fall, the phoenix sings,
Of life's mysteries, and all it brings.

So, listen closely, to the tarot's call,
For in its wisdom, lies answers for all.
With the phoenix as a guide, through shadows
and the light,
We journey onward, through day and night.

Wisdom

Under the cover of twilight's veil,
Beneath the moon's soft, silvery trail,
I met an owl, wise and old,
Perched upon a cloud's branch, serene and bold.

With eyes that gleamed like stars aglow,
He spoke in whispers soft and slow,
"Child of time, with worries deep,
Come, let me teach you how to keep
The precious gift of now, in sight,
To live in moments pure and bright."

He spread his wings, a regal sight,
And beckoned me to embrace the night.
"See," he said, "the worlds at rest,
Yet each heartbeat within your chest
Sings the anthem of life's sweet song,
A melody fleeting, yet ever strong."

"In every rustle of the leaves,
In every breeze that softly weaves
Through the tapestry of this earthly plane,
There lies a lesson, simple and plain:
To cherish each breath, each gentle breeze,
For in them lies life's mysteries."

He soared above, with grace untold,
A beacon of wisdom, ageless and bold.
And as I watched him fade from view,
His words sank deep, like morning dew.

So now, I strive to heed his call,
To embrace the present large and small.
For in the now, true joy is found,
In every sight, in every sound.

So let us learn from the wise old owl,
To savour each moment with heart and soul,
And dance in rhythm with life's flow,
In the timeless embrace of here and now.

Contemplation

Upon a cloud, I found my seat,
Above the world, where dreams retreat.
Looking down at the humdrum of life below,
A canvas vast, in constant flow.

With nimble fingers, I shaped the mist,
To craft a throne where thoughts persist.
In silent contemplation, I began to see,
The dance of life's complexity.

Below, humanity's hive did hum,
With routines set, their lives did run.
Each day a script, each moment planned,
In the maze of time, they're tightly fanned.

Beyond the clock's relentless chime,
Lies a rhythm, far from time.
In the whispers of the wind's caress,
In the beating heart's softness.

Life's essence breathes in the pause,
In the stillness between its laws.
It's in the moments when we stray,
From the path of habit's sway.

For there, amidst the silent air,
We find the truth we yearn to bear.
That life's not bound by hours and days,
But in the dance of endless ways.

So let us dare to step outside,
The confines where routine does hide.
And from the heights of clouds above,
Discover the beauty of life, and love.

Courage

In the clouds, where dreams take flight,
I found myself one starlit night,
At a tea party, whimsical and grand,
With unicorns and tales unplanned.

Beside me sat a creature rare,
A unicorn with silken hair,
With eyes that gleamed like opal stones,
And a mane that whispered ancient tones.

In riddles spoken of noble steed,
Of courage's flame, of daring deeds.
"Listen close," he said with a wink,
"As I pour courage into your drink."

With each sip, my fears did wane,
As he spoke of facing storms and rain.
"For courage lies not in the absence of fear,
But in the heart that holds it near."

He told of knights in Armour bright,
Who faced the darkness of the night,
Of maiden's fair with hearts so bold,
Their stories written in legends old.

"Courage," he said, "is not just might,
But the choice to stand in the face of fright.
To take a step, through trembling knees,
And chase the dreams that heartstrings tease."

As moonbeams danced and stars aligned,
I felt courage stir within my mind.
For in the company of unicorns and tea,
I found the courage to simply be.

Let us raise our cups high,
To courage found up in the cloudy sky.
And may we learn from riddles bold,
The lessons of courage as they unfold.

The beauty of the unknown

In this land where fairies flit and play,
And golden sunbeams light the way,
I wandered forth with heart aglow,
To where the unknown secrets grow.

Through enchanted forests, I did roam,
Each step a dance, each breath a poem.
For in the realm of the yet unseen,
Lies wonders, vast and evergreen.

In every glade, a mystery awaits,
In every whisper, a tale elates.
The magic of the unknown's sweet call,
Echoes through the forest tall.

To venture where the stars align,
And taste the nectar of the divine,
In realms where dreams are born anew,
And skies of gold stretch in view.

For in the embrace of the unknown's sway,
We find the spark to light our way,
Where possibilities bloom and soar,
And open hearts thirst for more.

So let us dance in the unknown's embrace,
And revel in its wondrous grace.
For in its depths, we'll find our homes,
Where dreams and fantasies freely roam.

Time

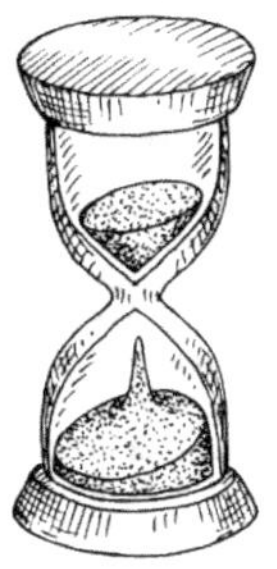

In whispers soft, I met a sprite,
Aerian, in the moon's pale light.
She spoke in riddles, wise and fair,
Guiding me through the misty air.

"Listen close," she said with glee,
"To learn the secret mystery.
In life's grand dance, what do you find?
Patience is key, to unwind."

Her wings aglow, a shimmering sight,
She posed a riddle in the night:
"I'm swift as breeze, yet slow as dawn,
In me, life's essence is truly drawn.

I wait for none, yet never rush,
In perfect time, I always hush.
What am I, in nature's play?
Trust me well, and you'll find your way."

I pondered long, with furrowed brow,
As the stars above began to bow.
Then like a whisper, clear and true,
The answer came, as the riddle grew:

"You are the river, flowing free,
From the mountain top to the endless sea.
You carve your path with patient grace,
Guiding all in your embrace."

Aerian smiled, her eyes alight,
In wisdom's glow, so pure and bright.
"Indeed," she said, "the river knows,
To trust in time, in ebb and flow."

"Like rivers, life unfolds its rhyme,
In perfect rhythm, over time.
Trust the current, let it be,
And you'll unlock life's mystery."

With that, she vanished into the night,
Leaving me with a newfound sight.
For in her riddles, I found a key,
To trust life's timing, and just be.

Tales from the ashes

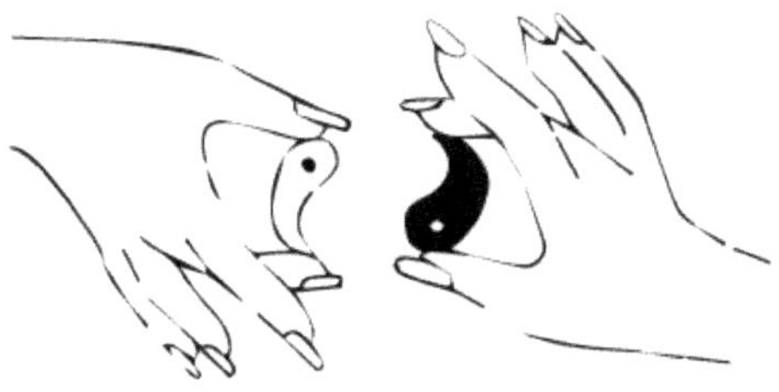

In twilight's hush, cruising into the fiery sky,
I beheld a phoenix, soaring high,
Its plumage ablaze with hues of gold,
In a sacred dance, this tale unfolds.

With wings outstretched, it took its flight
A beacon of hope in the fading light,
But as the sun dipped beyond horizon's gleam,
The phoenix descended in a fiery stream.

In a blaze of glory, it met its fate,
Consumed by flames, at destiny's gate,
Yet from the ashes, a whispering sigh,
A promise of rebirth, soaring high.

In dawn's embrace, a miracle unfurled,
As the phoenix rose, the ashes swirled,
In its resurrection, I found the key,
To embrace the transformation, and set myself
free.

For in every ending, a new beginning lies,
Like the phoenix, we too shall rise,
From the ashes of doubt, we'll find our way,
And soar into the dawn of a brand-new day.

Thud!

In the stillness of the night's embrace,
I stirred from dreams, in disarrayed grace.
A thunderous knock upon my door,
Echoed through the halls, to my very core.

With trembling hands and a racing heart,
I stumbled forth with a hesitant start.
The world outside seemed oddly real,
Yet shadows danced, a surreal feel.

As the door swung wide, reality tore,
And dreams dissolved, forevermore.
No floating clouds, no skyward flight,
Just the mundane world, devoid of light.

Yet in the moment, a truth revealed,
The adventure lives, through dreams concealed.
For in this world under sleep's embrace,
I found the courage to seek new space.

Though waking brought an end to flight,
The spirit soared in the dead of night.
And though the clouds may fade away high,
This dreamer's heart will always fly.

Pause

In the hustles fray, we tread our way,
Through mundane tasks in shades of grey.
But amidst the rush, a truth we find,
Life's beauty blooms in every kind.

Like flowers fair, in meadows vast,
Each moment gleams, a treasure amassed.
Yet in the grind, we often forget,
To pause, to savour, and not fret;

The fragrant scent of roses sweet,
Fill our soul with joy replete.
For life is but a fleeting dream,
A kaleidoscope, a vibrant stream.

Amidst the chaos, take a pause,
Embrace the whimsy, without cause.
For in the dance of everyday,
Beauty blossoms in its own array.

A sip of Life

In the morning's gentle light, I sit,
With a steaming mug, my spirits lift.
As coffee's warmth begins to seep,
I watch a bud, so softly creep.

Its petals tight, like secrets sealed,
Yet in its core, a world revealed.
I sip my coffee, watch in awe,
As nature crafts its tender law.

With every sip, a moment passed,
The bud unfurls, a dance so vast.
Each sip, a chapter, in its tale,
As life's true essence, is unveiled.

The orchid blooms, with grace untold,
A tale of beauty, to behold.
And in its bloom, I find a clue,
To life's deeper meaning, fresh and new.

Like coffee's warmth, love's gentle touch,
We open up, our souls to clutch.
Each day a sip, each moment shared,
Life's mysteries, we learn, we bare.

So, let us sip, and let us see,
The magic in each mystery.
For in a bud, in my coffee's steam,
The deeper meaning of life gleams.

Sunflowers

In vast lands, where sunlight weaves,
A tale of sunflowers, in quiet reprieve.
Their faces turned, towards the sun's embrace,
In each gentle sway, a lesson to trace.

They rise from the earth, with quiet grace,
Seeking light in every space.
Their stems, like soldiers, standing tall,
Teaching us to rise after every fall.

In their dance, with the sun, they find their way,
Bowing to dawn, bidding farewell to day.
Their resilience, a song in the breeze—
Whispering secrets through rustling leaves.

Through storms they bend, yet never break,

Resilience born from each sway they take.
Their petals, a symphony of hues,
Reminding us to embrace life's varied views.

And when their time upon this earth is done,
They bow their heads as if in gratitude to the
sun.
But in their seeds, new life awaits,
A cycle of hope that forever states:

That in the dance of Sun and Rain,
In the joys and sorrows that mark our gain,
We find in sunflowers, a timeless decree,
To bloom with grace, and to live free.

The dialogue

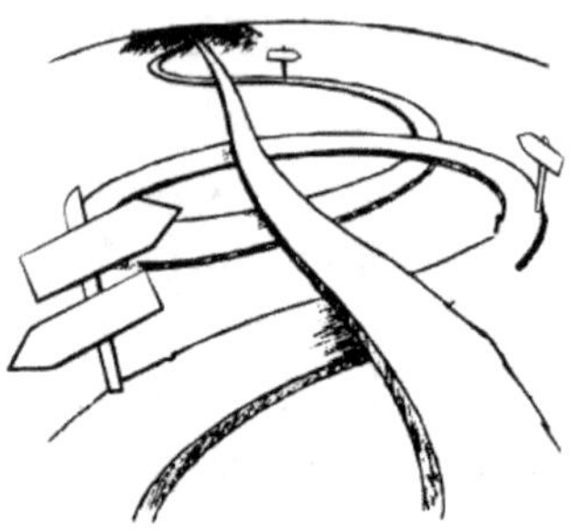

In a tea plantation, in twilight's gleam,
A girl with inked sunflower beams,
Beside her, in the haze, stands tall,
A bison wise, with eyes that call.

They meet amidst the misty air,
In whispered tones, they begin to share.
The girl, with petals etched on skin,
The bison, with wisdom deep within.

"Tell me," she asks, her voice a song,
"What is the purpose? Where do we belong?"
The bison, with a gentle nod,
Replies, "the answers lie beyond the sod."

"The meaning of life," the bison begins,
"Is found in moments, not in wins.
It's in the whispers of the breeze,
And in the rustle of the leaves.

It's in the laughter of a child at play,
And in the tears that mark our way.
It's in the bonds that tie us tight,
And in the stars that guide the night."

The girl with sunflowers in her eyes,
Listens, as the bison's wisdom flies.
In the dreamy haze of twilight's kiss,
They find the meaning, in moments of bliss.

And as the night begins to fall,
They part ways, but hear the call,
Of life's mysteries, ever deep,
In conversations, ethereal and sweet.

A guiding light

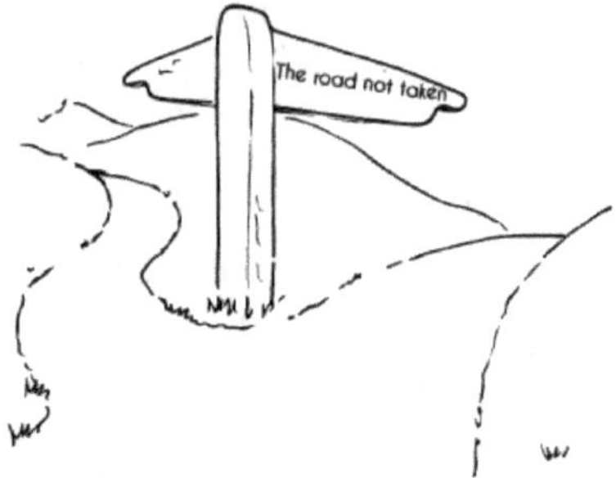

Under the Milky Way's lights, I set my stride,
On winding paths, where secrets hide.
Taking the long road, never alone,
With each step, a tale to be shown.

Along the way, a firefly gleams,
A luminescent beacon, in moonlit dreams.
With flickering light, he guides my way,
And in his glow, we begin to play.

"Come hither, traveller, " he softly sings,
In riddles and rhymes, he spreads his wings.
With each enigma, a puzzle to solve,
In his light, mysteries evolve.

As we walk, the night unfolds,
In wordplay and puns, our story rolls.
The firefly's light, a spark of delight,
Guiding me through this velvet night.

Through forests deep and meadows wide,
We journey on, side by side.
In laughter and jest, we while away,
The hours on this moonlit soiree.

And when at last, we reach the end,
The firefly bids farewell, my dear friend.
But in his light, I find my way,
Taking the long road home, at break of day.

For in the glow of the firefly's light,
I discovered joy, on a dark night.
And though our paths may now diverge,
In memory's embrace, we forever merge.

Live! Truly live

In life's grand play, courage is the key,
To seize the day, to be wild and free.
It takes guts and grit, to face the strife,
And embark on adventures, in the journey of
life.

Like a lion's roar, courage calls,
To break free from fears, from doubts and stalls.
It's the fuel that ignites, the flame within,
To chase after dreams, to rise and win.

With each step forward, courage blooms,

Like a flower in spring, dispelling glooms.
It's the wind in your sails, the fire in your soul,
Pushing you forward, to reach your goal.

So, take a leap, don't hesitate,
Embrace the challenge, don't underestimate.
For in the face of fear, courage stands tall,
Guiding you through, to conquer it all.

With bravery as your shield, and valour as your
guide,
You'll conquer mountains, you'll reach the tide.
For in this tapestry of life, courage weaves,
A tale of triumph, for all who believe.

Impermanence

In whispers from the ancient lands,
Where tales of Gods and mortals stand.
Mythology weaves its tales,
Of impermanence, where all else seems pale.

Through Brahma's breath, creations start,
But even he must play his part.
For time is relentless, its ceaseless flow,
And all that is born must one day go.

Vishnu, the preserver, steady and true,
Embraces change in all he does.
For in his hands, the universe will sway,
Impermanence, its price to pay.

Shiva, the destroyer, fierce and bold,

In his dance, impermanence is told.
For in destruction, new life springs,
In every ending, a new cycle begins.

In tales of Krishna, sweet and wise,
Impermanence in love's disguise.
For even in his divine embrace,
Mortality finds its rightful place.

And in these lessons from ancient verse,
Impermanence, a truth, something to rehearse.
For life is a fleeting, transient song,
In its ebb and flow, we all belong.

Love

In the still night, by my window pane,
A nightingale sings, a haunting refrain.
Its melody whispers, a tale untold,
Of love's journey, from darkness to gold.

From the depths of Hades, where shadows
dwell,
Comes a lesson of love, a story to tell,
For in the underworld's embrace, a love did
ignite,
A bond eternal, in darkness' sight.

Hades, the lord, with a heart of stone,
Found solace in Persephone's beauty alone.
In the depths of darkness, their love did bloom,
A union profound, in the kingdom of gloom.

For in love's embrace, darkness fades away,
And even in Hades' realm, love finds its way.
In the silence of night, their whispers entwine,
A love eternal, in shadows divine.

So let the nightingale sing, let its songs be heard,
A tale of love, from Hades' underworld.
For even in darkness, love's light shines bright,
Guiding us through the shadows, into the deep
night.

Forgiveness

When tempests rage and oceans wildly churn,
I watch as man, in arrogance, does tread,
Upon my soil, with selfish hearts that yearn,
To claim dominion, as my tears are shed.

Yet still, I stand, in patient, silent grace,
Forgiving wounds inflicted by mankind,
For in my vast embrace, there lies no trace
Of vengeance, only love, so pure and kind.

Yet as I watch, with sorrow deep and wide,
Man's heart grows heavy with each petty slight,
Forgiveness falters, buried deep inside,
Lost in the shadows of pride's stubborn fight.

Oh, why do you, my children, fail to see?
That forgiveness sets your spirit free!

The golden key

In the darkest pits, where shadows dare to dwell,
Forgiveness lurks, a tale to tell.
In the abyss of pain, where demons reign,
Forgiveness whispers, amidst the bane.

In the echoes of torment, where screams
resound,
Forgiveness emerges, from underground.
In the heart of despair, where hope is slain,
Forgiveness blooms, amidst the pain.

In the void of hatred, where vengeance thrives,
Forgiveness dares, where darkness dives.
In the abyss of sin, where guilt resides,
Forgiveness offers a chance to rise.

In the depths of darkness, where souls decay
Forgiveness beckons, to light the way.
For in forgiveness, there lies release,
From the shackles of darkness, it grants peace.

In the darkest of dark hours, when all seems lost,
Embrace forgiveness, no matter the cost.
For in its embrace, there lies the golden key,
To set your spirit, forever free.

The girl with the sunflower tattoo

In the silence of the night, where shadows creep,
There stands a girl with secrets buried deep.
Her skin a canvas, tells a tale untold,
Of gratitude in whispers, and mysteries so bold.

Upon her arm, a sunflower bloom,
Its petals vibrant, casting out all gloom.
A tattoo etched in ink, yet far alive,
A beacon of gratitude, where shadows strive.

For in her eyes, the sunflowers glow,
Reflects a journey few will ever know.
Each petal speaks of trials overcome,
Each leaf a testament to battles won.

In moments dark, when all seems lost
She turns to gratitude, no matter the cost.
For in its embrace, she finds her light,
Guiding her through the darkest night.

So let the world marvel at her tattoo's hue,
A symbol of gratitude, strong and true.
For in the girl with the sunflower art,
Resides a spirit grateful, from the heart.

Timeless Love

Amidst the fragrant blooms of jasmine bright,
Where the Ganges whispers tales of love anew,
I found your gaze beneath the moon's soft light,
A sacred bond in shades of twilight hue.

Oh, Romeo, my heart, my sacred flame,
In courtyards where the peacocks dance with
grace,
Your name, a mantra, whispers, without shame,
In every prayer, I seek your gentle face.

Though time may strive to keep us apart,
Our love, like rivers flow, defying the land,
Unyielding as the ancient banyan's heart,
Together, we will take our destined stand.

In Mother Earth's embrace, our love will soar,
Two souls entwined, forever, evermore.

The Dancer

In temples where lamps alight,
A dancer's form takes life in rhythmic grace,
Each step, a prayer, each gesture pure delight,
Her movements weave devotion's timeless lace.

Adorned in silk, with anklets in silver that
chime,
She dances for the Goddess, divine muse,
Her eyes ablaze, transcending space and time,
At every turn, the heavens she pursues.

Oh, Bharatnatyam dancer, radiant and true,
Your feet beat ancient rhythms on the ground,
With every arch, with every leap anew,
The cosmic tales of deities resound.

Your art, a bridge from earthly to divine,
In dance, you honour all that is sublime.

Ballad of the Bloom

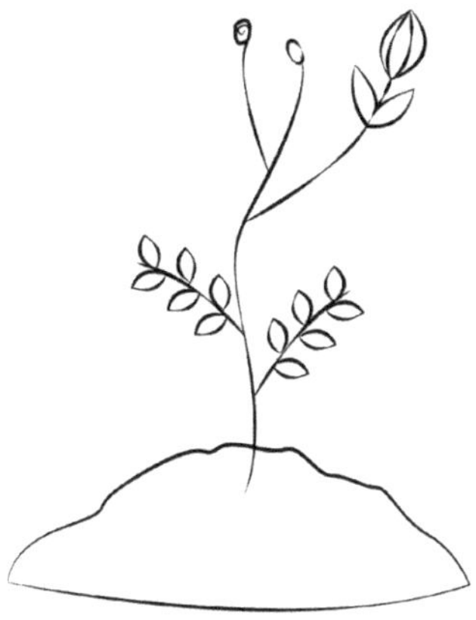

In her garden of blooms, where sunlight plays
A tender bloom slowly says,
Of a girl who comes to visit everyday
With a heart so pure, in every way.

"She waters me with gentle hands,
Her hands, a blessing from the skies,
With kindness that the angels planned,
And songs that make my petals shine.

Her voice, a melody so sweet,
It dances on the morning breeze,
Each note a promise, soft and sweet,
That brings my soul a gentle ease.

Her laughter is a golden stream,
That flows and sparkles in the light,
Her eyes, like stars, forever gleam,
And chase away the darkest night.

She sings of love and dreams so high,
Her garden blooms with every word,
Beneath the vast and humbling sky,
Her songs of joy are always heard.

Oh, if the world could see her grace,
And know the kindness she imparts,
In every flower's smiling face,
Would bloom the beauty of her heart.

So here I stand, a humble bloom,
In this enchanted, sacred plot,
Her love dispels all trace of gloom,
With every care, with every thought.

In every petal, every leaf,
Her gentle spirit does abide,
For she, the girl, who sings belief,
Is beauty and kindness glorified."

Home

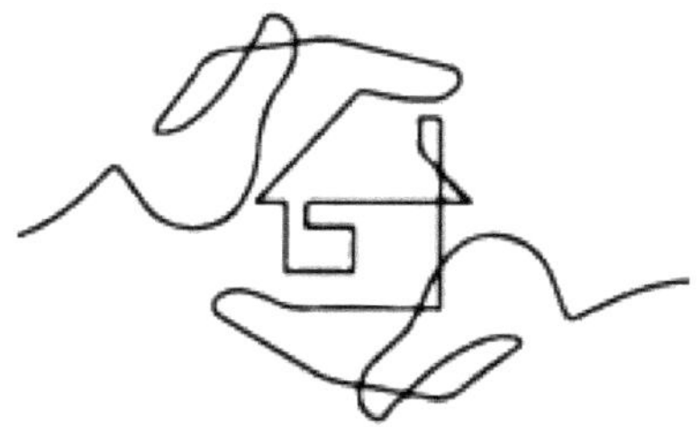

Home, where the misty mountains rise,
A heaven draped in green, where dreams reside,
Beneath your skies, so wide and wise,
In nature's arms, with grace, we bide.

Amidst your hills where tea leaves gently sway,
The bison roam with strength and silent pride,
Their shadows dance at the break of day,
In valleys deep and mountains wide.

The bears amble through dappled light,
In search of berries sweet and honey gold.
With careful steps through day and night,
Their stories in your woods unfold.

Porcupines with quills so sharp and fine,
Wander through the under-bush unseen,
In twilight hours, their paths align,
With whispers of the forest green.

Panthers on the prowl with elegance and might,
Their eyes like embers in the evenings glow,
Silent hunters in the velvet night,
Their presence felt where shadows flow.

In Coonoor's heart, the artisans create,
Cheese so nice, with flavours deep and true,
Tea that tells of history's fate,
And chocolate sweet as morning dew.

Homegrown berries yield their fragrant wine,
A taste of sunlit days and starry eves,
In every sip, the moments shine,
Of laughter shared beneath the leaves.

Dear Coonoor, your life, a symphony,
Where wild and tame in harmony align,
A paradise where hearts are free,
In every sip of tea and wine.

From bear's to bison's, to the panther's stealthy
grace,
To porcupines and plantation tales that
intertwine,
Your beauty, time can't erase,
Coonoor, your essence is a song,
In you, my heart will forever belong.

Ayyah (Grandfather)

Ayyah, with hands so kind and true,
Your goodness—a deep and endless ocean's hue,
In every act, lessons you did impart,
Of equity and love, a boundless art.

In your embrace, we found a sacred space,
Where kindness flourished, and compassion was
more than a face.
You taught us through your deeds, so pure and
grand,
To help the needy with a benevolent hand.

Your stories, filled with wisdom, old and wise,
Reflected in your warm and gentle eyes,
You spoke of actions, of keeping your word,
You showed us how to live with love and not
follow the herd.

In the busy streets, corridors and grand halls,
Your presence brought calm that still enthrals,
You treated every soul with equal care,
In every gesture, justice was laid bare.

From grand dinners to private home soirees,
From giving alms to ensuring no one around you
had to pay.
You wove a tapestry of love so wide,
In every thread, your spirit does reside.

Ayyah, your life was a beacon bright,
Guiding us through the darkest nights
With hands that gave and a heart so vast,
Your legacy in us will forever last.

We honour you and every righteous deed,
In every heart you've planted a kind seed,
Your lessons of equality and love,
Will guide us till we meet in realms above.

Grandfather, with love I sing your praise,
In every breath, your memory stays,
A gentle giant with a noble heart,
In every moment, your teachings will never part.

Dancing Feet

In Bengal's land where rivers softly flow,
There dwells a soul with a heart so pure and
kind,
A footballer whose grace and spirit show,
The strength and wisdom of a Shiva mind.

With every stride upon the field so vast,
You dance as Nataraja, fierce and free.
In moments swift, both future and past
Converge in your symphony.

Your heart blossoms and blooms with each play,
In acts of Kindness, rivals you disarm,
With every pass, the crowd's cheers softly sway.
As they feel your gentle spirit's charm.

In you, a power does flow,
A force so strong, yet calm and true.
With every goal, your love for life bestows,
Bringing joy to all who watch and view.

Oh, dearest one, your teachings do inspire,
A lesson in humility and grace,
Like Shiva's dance, you set my heart afire,
In your embrace, I find my sacred place.

Together, let us walk this path of light,
With you, my love, the world feels ever right.

Beyond Bus Rides

On the RSR town bus, the lessons flow,
A comedy of errors, a hilarious show,
From crowded aisles to bumpy rides,
Here are the truths that life and bus rides
provide!

Patience is virtue, they say,
But on a bus, it is tested every day,
As you wait in a serpentine queue,
Just to squeeze in like a sardine, it's true!

Personal space is a myth!
On a bus, you're in for a tight-knit riff,
With elbows jabbing and knees knocking,
You'll soon forget what it means to be walking.

Negotiation skills are key,
When the conductor demands a fee,
But you only have a few notes!
So, you bargain or wait for change.

Balance is crucial, my friend,
On curves and turns, it's hard to pretend,
That you're not swaying like a palm in the
breeze,
Holding on for dear life, if you please.

Diversity is everywhere,
On an Indian bus, you'll find it laid bare
From chatty aunties to silent stares,
Each journey brings a cast of characters.

Laughter is the best remedy,
When chaos reigns supreme, it sets you free,
So next time you board the local town bus,
Remember these lessons and enjoy your next
ride without any fuss.

Sitar Saga

In strings of the sitar, melodies entwine,
A timeless dance of raga and rhyme,
In every note, a tale divine.

Beneath the moonlit sky, stars align,
As fingers weave a tapestry sublime,
In strings of sitar, melodies entwine.

With every pluck, emotions intertwine,
A journey through the heart's labyrinth,
In every note, a tale divine.

The soul of the divine in each string,
A symphony of culture, so enthralling
In strings, ragas take form and meaning divine.

Through joy and sorrow, love and decline,
The sitars strings, sing a song endless in time,
In every note, a tale divine

Let the music weave its spell so fine,
As our spirits soar and intertwine,
In its strings, we hear melodies divine.

Divine Devi

In every woman, a goddess resides,
With strength and grace, she bravely strides,
Like Devi Durga, fierce and bold,
She faces challenges, her spirit untold.

In her nurturing embrace, like Devi Lakshmi's
grace,
She brings abundance and love to every space,
With wisdom deep, like Devi Saraswathi's lore,
She inspires minds and opens every door.

In her resilience, like Devi Kalis might,
She conquers darkness, embracing light,
With compassion vast, like Devi Parvathi's care,
She nurtures the soul with tender flair.

Oh woman, embodiment of divine energy,
In feminine energy, we find the essence of
eternity,
With every stride, the essence is divine,
Divine Devi, let your light shine.

Dear Caterpillar

Dear Caterpillar, with legs so many,
Your journey ahead may seem a bit zany,
But fret not, my friend, don't feel like a chump,
For patience is the key, don't be a grump!

Just hang in there, don't be a creep,
Soon you'll emerge from your cocoon's sleep,
And when you do, you'll spread your wings
wide,
No longer a caterpillar, but a butterfly—tender
and bright!

So, chin up, Princess, you won't stay a larva,
Your transformation will be quite the art canvas,
Just keep your cool, and trust in fate,
You'll soon be soaring, it's worth the wait!

With fluttery wings and colours so bright,
You'll dance in the breeze, a magnificent sight,
And as you flutter through the flowery glade,
Patience, you will learn amidst every leaf blade!

A thorny tale

Oh rose, so fair, so lovely to behold,
With petals soft with hues of pink and red,
You bask in sunlight, while I remain cold,
A thorn, forgotten, on your stem instead.

Yet do not mock me, for I play my part,
Though sharp and prickly, I have my charm,
For without me, your beauty would depart,
You are protected by my prickly, thorny arm.

While you are praised for your sweet perfume,
And poets sing of your romantic grace,
I stand here, in the shadows of your bloom,
A humble thorn, with a less glamorous face.

But let us jest, for in the floral scene,
A rose without a thorn? Quite absurd, I deem!

Plea for Peace

My beloved children, hear my voice echoing
through the winds,
Rustling through the leaves and murmuring in
the rivers.
I am your Mother Earth, the giver of life,
The keeper of souls, and I come to you with a
plea from the depths of my heart.

In the midst of the horror that plagues your
world,
I see the violence, the bombs,
The greed that tears at the fabric of your
existence.
 My heart aches with every explosion,
Every cry of pain, every act of cruelty.
I weep for the lives lost, for the innocence
shattered,
For the scars that mar your souls.

Amidst the darkness, there is still hope.
There is still a flicker of light that can guide you
Back to your path of peace and harmony.
I urge you,
My children, to listen to that inner voice,
To embrace love and compassion, and reject;
Temptation of power and greed.

For when you sow seeds of hatred, you reap
only destruction.
When you wield weapons of war, you sow only
seeds of sorrow.
But when you open your hearts to love,
When you extend a hand of friendship, when
you embrace each other,
You plant seeds of peace and harmony.

I call upon you to put down your weapons, lay
aside your differences.
And come together as one family, heal your past
wounds.
Build a future of dignity and respect. Let us
nurture the planet,
Let us cherish the diversity that enriches our
lives.

My children, the power to create a world of
peace and harmony lies within each of you.

Join hands and work together to make that
vision a reality.
For only then will my heart truly sing,
and only then will I see my children living in
harmony,
With each other and with the world around.

Morning Coffee

In the quiet dawn, before the sun does rise,
My heart yearns for you, my cherished prize.
From the hills of Coorg to the Kerala plains,
Your rich aroma breaks my sleep's chain.

In a brass pot on a gentle flame,
You are made with great care, in this morning
game.
With a hint of ginger and a dash of jaggery.
You awaken my senses and make my insides
fluttery.

My Coffee, in this earthen cup,
Each golden drop, I gratefully sip,
You bring the vigour, you spark the cheer,
Banishing shadows, erasing fear.

From the bustling markets to the temples serene,
You are the pulse of the daily routine

From Kanyakumari's streets to Kashmir's nooks
Your essence is found in every souk.

My Kaapi, in the first lights gleam,
You weave through my thoughts like a sacred
dream.
With each blessed sip, my spirit ascends,
To you, my companion, my heartfelt amends.

From Rajasthani deserts to the coastal bay
Your magic lingers, at the start of each day
In every game, with every prayer,
Your presence is felt, vibrant and rare.

Here is to you, my morning grace,
With a thankful heart, I embrace your place.
In the rhythm of my routine both old and new,
My morning coffee, I owe much to you!

Monsoon Magic

The heavens break, a whisper in the night,
And monsoons sweep with symphonies of rain.
In each drop's fall, the earth receives its light,
A rhythmic dance that soothes the heart's pain.

Oh, listen to the ragas of the storm,
The melodies that nature's breath reveals.
In every note, the clouds and winds transform,
And with their song, the wounded spirit heals.

The peacocks cry, the tabla's deep refrain,
The sitar's strings, the thunder's wild embrace,
In harmony, they weave a sweet refrain,
A timeless tune, a lover's soft embrace.

As Keats penned, so too the monsoons sing,
In Ragas old, where emotion and nature cling.

Rendezvous with Ragas

In Bhairav's dawn, the red sunlight, we see
In the morning's blush, our hearts ignite, amidst
an endless sea.

 Todi's gold at noon, a warm embrace
A midday glow, our spirits light and full of
grace.

In Desh's rain, the green earth sighs anew,
Its emerald notes in fresh delight.

As Yaman's twilight paints the sky blue,
A tranquil peace in fading light amidst the
evening hue.

Kafis dusk in lavender and grey,
It invites words that are left unsaid, along the
way.

Kedar's night, a deep and velvet black,
In starry notes, our dreams take flight taking us
beyond all we think we lack.

Bageshrees hues of moonlit night,
In silver songs, pure love's insight.

Raga Hamsadhwani, morning's pure white light,
Its notes like lilies, calm and bright.

Bhairavi's crimson evening fire,
In every flame, a desire to inspire.

In megh's monsoon, shades of silver-gray.
A dance of clouds, the thunders might be on full
display.

Darbari's depth, in indigo profound,
A royal hue, with echoes that resound.

In Marwa's sunset, orange hues flow,
A dusk where light and dark unite and glow.

Rageshrees blush, the pink of evening blooms,
In every petal, the purity of love looms.

In musical hues, a symphony of life,
In every note, the world's own light.

Every colour, every sound, a story untold.
In Mother Earth's canvas, magic unfolds.

In music notes, our spirits lift.
In nature's notes, our souls delight.

A Memory in Ruin

In days of old, a home stood proud and tall,
Its walls adorned with memories so dear.
But now, in ruins, it begins to fall,
A silent witness to the passage of years.

Once filled with laughter, joy and love's
embrace,
Now echoes silence, a mournful song.
The grandeur fades, no more its former grace,
As time erodes the place where we belonged.

The halls that echoed with our footsteps sound,
Now lie in stillness empty and bare.
Each room, a stage where life's scenes were
found,
Now whispers tales of splendour lost to air.

Gone are the days of warmth beside the fire,
Where stories flowed like rivers deep and wide.
The laughter fades, replaced by quiet mire,
As shadows cloak the home where love once
thrived.

The garden blooms no more with vibrant hues.
Wilted flowers and petals on the ground.
The trees in silence, mourning what they lost,
Their branches reaching for the past unbound.

Oh, magnificent home, now lost to time's cruel
hand,
Your memory lingers like a haunting dream.
Though you may crumble, your spirit will
withstand,
In hearts and minds, you'll forever gleam.
Once full of life, oh home so bright,
Now echoes faint of lost delight,
Its fire gone, a darkened sight,
Now a whisper like the endless night.

Dancing Delight

In the heart of glistening meadows, beneath the
monsoon skies
Where the raindrops kiss the earth in sweet
embrace,
There, amidst the symphony of nature's sighs,
Behold the peacock, adorned with sovereign
grace.

With feathers spread like a painter's vibrant hue,
She strides upon the dampened earth with pride,
Her iridescent plumes, a kaleidoscope anew,
Reflecting the essence of creation's tide.

In each flicker of her tail, a story unfolds,
A narrative of life, birth and rebirth,
As if the cosmos, in her dance, it beholds,
A sacred rhythm that transcends the bounds of
earth.

With each step, she weaves a tapestry divine,
A dance that mirrors the cosmic energy flow,
In the rhythm of the rain, her movements align,
With the heartbeat of the world, her colours
glow.

Oh, how the heavens sing with her sway,
Clouds joining this ballet,
And the earth, in reverence bows to this display,
The peacock's divine serenade.

Enraptured by these spins and twirls,
A testament to the beauty of creation's design,
In this dance, a divine force unfurls,
And we glimpse into the eternal, in the rains and
soft sunshine.

Red Boots

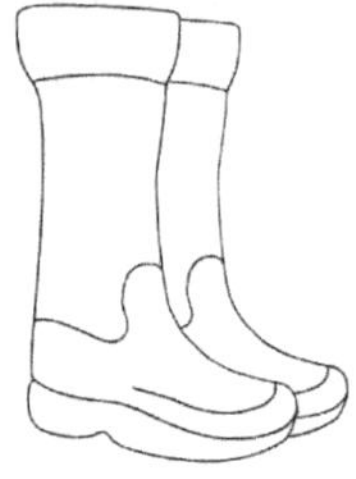

In my closet, hidden away. Lies a pair of red
boots,
Once snug and bold, now abandoned, they no
longer fit,
They were my strides companion, my flairs
delight,
But time has passed, and now they gather dust,
Memories cling to their worn leather, a
bittersweet echo,
Of days when they adorned my feet with grace.

Each step a dance in my vibrant red boots,
But seasons change, leaving behind an echo
Of dreams outgrown, of paths where they no
longer fit,
Now relegated to the corner, covered in dust,
Their former glory but a distant delight.

I remember the days when they were a delight,
When every strut was a testament to their grace,

But now they sit forgotten, covered in dust,
Those once-beloved, eye-catching red boots,
In my closet, a symbol of what no longer fits,
A silent reminder of a faded echo.

The silence now fills the room with echo,
A silent lament for that lost delight,
For the times when they were the perfect fit,
And I moved through life at a steady pace,
But now they gather dust, those red boots,
Their vibrant hue dulled by the passage of time.

Perhaps it's time to let go, to leave behind the
dust,
To bid farewell to those red boots, their echo,
For clinging to what no longer fits brings no
delight,
It's time to release them with love and grace,
To make space for new journeys and new boots
to sit.
And cherish the memories of where they once
fit.

Farewell, dear boots, with your echo of grace,
Though no longer fitting, you were once my
delight,
Now covered in dust, in the corner you sit,
Adieu, dear boots, it's time for a new fit!

Strength

In the heart of the forest, where trees stand tall,
Amidst the whispers of leaves and the song of
the thrush,
I wandered lost, burdened by the weight of it all,
Seeking solace, seeking refuge, in nature's
gentle hush.

The world around me seemed to spin out of
control,
Troubles and worries like a tempest in my mind,
But in the embrace of the woods, I found a
guiding soul,
A silent witness to the beauty I longed to find.

With each step, the earth beneath me whispered secrets,
Of resilience, endurance, of life's endless flow,
The river, a steady companion, murmured reassurances,
As it danced over stones, with a graceful rhythmic glow.

In the dance of sunlight filtering through the leaves,
I glimpsed hope, a beacon in the midst of despair,
For in nature's vastness, my soul found reprieve,
And the burdens that weighed me down, I began to bear.

The wind became an ally, carrying away my fears,
As I stood on the edge of a cliff, gazing at the horizon,
The mountains loomed majestic, wiping away my tears,
And in their towering presence, I found my strength to carry on.

For nature is a teacher, a healer, a friend,
In its hug, I found the courage to face my strife,

And though the journey ahead may twist and
bend,
I walk with newfound strength, renewed by
nature's life.

Love, Death

In the deep dark, where whispers fade,
I linger, unseen, in this masquerade.
I'm the silent guest at greed's grand parade.

Beneath the glimmer of treasures amassed,
I dwell, in the shadows, my presence masked.
In the heart of greed, I'm eternally cast.

They chase elusive dreams, their desire
unbound,
In their pursuit, my whispers resound.
But in the end, it's my embrace they've found.

They hoard their wealth, their treasures arrayed,
Yet in their grasp, they find only shade.
For in the arms of greed, I've long stayed.

I am the answer to every truth left unsaid,
I'm greed's kingdom, I am both fear and dread.
In my silent embrace, they find their bed.

Listen closely to the secrets I've relayed,
In every shadow, I'm quietly laid.
For in this world of greed, I am death, a
serenade of peace.

Trusting Time

In shattered fragments, heartbreak's cruel
decree,
But from the pieces, new strength shall soon set
you free.

Through tear-stained nights, in anguish deep,
Emerges resilience, from pain's cruel keep.
Though scars may linger, wounds slowly heal,
In time, the heart finds its rhythm, amidst a
stormy sea.

Trust the universe, its mysterious ways,
It guides our paths through our darkest days.
For every goodbye holds a hidden gift,
In endings, new beginnings swiftly lift.

Embrace the journey, with open arms,
For even in chaos, loves magic charms.
In the stillness of dawn, a promise is made,
That love will find us, not to evade.

For when we least expect, it gently appears,
True love's embrace, to calm our fears.

So, let go of doubts, let go of your fears,
In the universal dance, our soul steers.
Through heartbreak's trials, we learn to soar,
To find true love, forevermore.

Sweet Respite

Softly sighs the weary soul, seeking rest,
Where shadows dance in twilight's gentle crest,
Each fleeting moment, a balm to the heart,
Easing the burdens that tear us apart.
Tender whispers of solace, like gentle streams,
Relinquishing worries, embracing dreams.
Endless peace, in the hush of the night,
Soothing the spirit, in its quiet flight.
Prayers whispered softly, to the stars above.
In sweet respite, we find solace and love.
Time pauses gently, in this sacred space,
Ephemeral bliss, in each fleeting embrace.

A Cart

Upon a dusty country road in heat so fierce,
A humble cart, in structure strong and true,
Under the magnificent sun, with rays that pierce,
You offered shade, a blissful, cooling hue.

Your wooden wheels creaked gently, soft and
slow,
As if to sing a lullaby of peace.
In the sweltering noon's relentless, fiery glow,
Your shaded haven granted sweet release.

Beneath your canopy, I found my rest,
A moment's pause from toil and weary tread.
The bull's eyes with patience manifest,
Their steadfast strength, in quiet beauty spread.

Oh, simple cart, your gift I'll ne'er forget,
In scorching times, your solace eased my sweat.

Tale of a Brew

Here lies the tale of a brew sublime,
A perfect cup that met a tragic time.
With leaves so fine and water just right,
It was set to be a drinker's delight.

Born of patience, steeped with care,
A blend so perfect, beyond compare.
Yet destiny played its cruel, swift part,
And left this tea with a heavy heart.

Perhaps it was a doorbell's ring,
Or a child's unexpected swing.
Maybe a call that wouldn't end,
Or an email sent by a pesky friend.

The steam rose up, a fragrant sigh,
As moments passed, it wondered why.
Untouched, un-sipped, it sat alone,
A masterpiece to never be known.

We laugh and cry for what could be,
A cup of joy, now history.
Let us raise our mugs, in spirit at least,
To this noble brew, a fallen feast.

For though it never met the lip,
Or had the chance to take a sip,
Its memory will linger on,
In every brew, at every dawn.

Here's to a tea that met its fate,
A cup of great taste, truly great.
Unconsumed, but never gone,
Your legacy, forever drawn.

Dear Home

On ancient walls, I've marked the passing time,
In every tick, a story etched sublime,

Your corridors have echoed laughter's song,
The harmony of chatter, through your hallways
still throng.

The rain has danced upon your weathered face,
While sunshine once kissed your eaves with
grace.
The children's footsteps pitter-pat and fade
away,
The memories remain, Oh, Time! How you
play!

The gatherings, the feasts, the festive cheer you
spread,
I recall those moments, but the future I dread!

Through joys and sorrows, a silent witness I
have been,
A keeper of your tales and all I have seen.
Now as my hands move slower, still I speak to
you,
Of all we've shared, the moments surreal but
true!
Dear ancient walls, I've marked the passing
time.
You served them well, for you now I chime.

Roadside Lotus

In the roadside gutter, where shadows play,
A lotus blooms, defiant, in the clay.
Magnificent, it rises from the grime,
A silent witness to the passage of time.

The mud, a cradle of forgotten dreams,
Holds secrets in its dark, polluted streams.
Yet from this muck, a flower pure, unsoiled,
Emerges, its beauty unspoiled.

Petals, like whispers of a secret prayer,
Unfurl in the heavy, stagnant air.
Each one a testament to silent strife,
To the quiet persistence of life.

The road beside it, rough and worn,
Echoes with footsteps, hurried and forlorn.
But the lotus stands, a beacon bright,
In the desolate landscape, a soft light.

Oh, how it mocks the filth below,
With every graceful measure you grow.
A symbol of purity, against the odds,
A reminder of forgotten Gods.

In its reflection, the sky and mud merge,
A poignant hymn, a quiet dirge.
Magnificent lotus, bloom on and on,
In your fragile beauty, night and dawn.

You teach us, in your silent stance,
Of resilience and the cosmic dance.
In the dirtiest waters, you find your place,
An emblem of grace in a graceless space.

Biriyani

In the kitchen's warmth, where love is stirred,
A symphony of flavours, without a word.
Fragrant rice, each grain a tale,
Of ancient lands and a spice-filled trail.

Cinnamon whispers secrets from afar,
While cloves add depth, a culinary star.
Cardamom sings with a sweet refrain,
In this pot where spices mix and wane.

Saffron threads, like golden dreams,
Infuse the dish with vibrant gleams.
Turmeric bright as the midday sun,
In this lover's dance, all ingredients are one.

Tender meat marinated with care,
Absorbs the essence, flavours laid bare.
Ginger garlic, a pungent embrace,
Adding depth to the dish's grace.

As onions caramelise to sweet gold,
They tell of passions, hot and bold.
Tomatoes burst with love's sweet nectar,
Binding each grain like a protector.

Yoghurt smooth, like warm sunshine,
Softens the heat where chilies lie,
Mint and coriander, fresh and green,
A hint of cool in the spicy sheen.

Layer by layer this pot is built,
With love and patience, every spice split.
Steam rises, carrying the scent,
Of a love profound, with every moment spent.

In the pot, a story unfolds,
Of love and flavours, rich and bold.
Each bite, a journey to a distant land,
Crafted with heart and loving hands.

As this biriyani simmers and cooks,
The aroma like a spice souk.
A feast of passion, on a humble plate,
In flavours, love we celebrate.

From the Glow

In the flickering glow, the candle gives its light,
A lesson learned in sacrifice and might,
It burns itself to make the darkness bright.
Its wax diminishes throughout the night,
Yet steadfast, it shines, no thought but to be
bright.,
In a flickering glow, the candle gives its light.

For other's sight, it bears this fiery plight,
A testament to what's truly above ordinary sight,
It burns itself to make the darkness bright!

Each drip of wax, a tale of quiet might,
Of giving all, a silent, gentle fight,
In a flickering glow, the candle gives its light.

It stands alone, a beacon in the night,
Teaching us to serve, and spread the light.
It burns itself to make the darkness bright.

So, from this flame, we learn to love what's
right,
To always choose to spread the light.
And know that we can make the darkness bright.

Dance Anklets

Dear dance anklets, with jingles pure and bright,
You bore my steps, each twist and turn you
knew,
In every move, you made the dance ignite.

Through rhythmic beats, you held on with all
your might,
Supporting every leap, I dared to do
Dear anklets, with jingles pure and bright.

Your tiny bells, like stars in the night,
Echoed the joy and sorrows I danced through,
In every move, you made the dance ignite.

Though worn and scuffed, you never showed
your plight,
Bearing the abuse, remaining true,
Oh, dance anklets, with jingles pure and bright.

For every bruise and strain, your silent fight,
Enduring all, your strength I always drew,
In every move, you made the dance ignite.

With a grateful heart, I thank you for the light,
For all you did, and all you helped me pursue,
Oh, dear anklets, with jingles pure and bright,
In every move, you made the dance ignite.

Love & Sorrow

On the funeral ghat, sorrow flows deep.
And love blooms in silence, where shadows
weep.

Amidst the chants and the sacred flames,
Two hearts find solace, shedding old names.

In the flicker of pyres, a tender light
Love's gentle whisper in the heart of night.

Ashes to ashes, life's cycle spins,
Yet love finds beauty, where death begins.

The river flows, carrying tales untold,
Of love that sparkles in sorrows' fold.

In the scent of sandalwood, bittersweet,
Love and loss in harmony meet.

Grief's heavy veil and joy's soft grace,
Dance together in this sacred space.

For life's true essence, a delicate art,
Balancing love and sorrow in every heart.

On the funeral ghat, where tears and prayers
start,
Love also finds its echo, in the stillness of the
heart.

Blessings

In the hush of dawn, a whisper spreads across
the skies.
Golden hues emerge as the night bids soft
goodbyes.

The horizon blushes in a tender, warm embrace,
Painting dreams anew on morning's gentle face.

Stars retreat in silence, yielding to the light,
Heaven's glow awakens, chasing off the night.

First rays of the sun, like fingers touch the earth,
Breathing life into shadows, heralding rebirth.

Mountains stand in reverence, cloaked in amber
haze,
Nature holds its breath, enraptured by the blaze.

Birds compose their hymns, a chorus sweet and
clear,
In the sacred stillness, the divine draws near.

Waves adorned with sparkles kiss the waiting
shore,
Whispers of the cosmos, stories from ancient
folklore.

Petals softly open, bathed in golden streams,
Morning dew illuminates the night's dreams.

A symphony of colours, each a divine phrase,
Heaven's art unveiled in dawn's resplendent
gaze.

The world awakes in wonder, bathed in holy
light,
Witness the miracle that unfolds each night.

In this sacred moment, hearts with joy align,
Watching dawn's arrival, touched by the divine.

Words Unsaid

In silent glances, words we never say,
Lie bonds unspoken, strong as rooted trees.
Like moon and tide in nature's endless play,
We find our balance, carried by the breeze.

The flowers turn their faces to the sun,
Dependant on the light, yet speak no vow aloud.
In quiet grace, their lives and ours are spun,
By unseen threads, of which we both are proud.

The river's flow carves the steadfast stone,
Each shaped by time, in mutual embrace.
So too our hearts, in silence, find their tone,
A harmony that neither can displace.

Creations web, so intricate and fine,
Reflects the silent bond that nature defines.
In life's hustle, what's left unsaid,
Is what the soul is longing to be fed.

Dancing God

In Mother Nature's soul, the dance of Nataraja
flows,
Through this sacred dance, the cosmic rhythm
grows.

With each step, the universe sways and bends,
Creations pulse with every beat it sends.

Flames encircle, dispelling the shadows that
creep,
In this divine play, the world's essence spreads
far and deep.

Destruction and rebirth merge in each pose,,
Life and death, through Nataraja's grace,
juxtapose.

The universal pulse like a mystic drumbeat,
Creating moments for light and darkness to
meet.

Eyes closed, but ever seeing,
In dance, an eternal truth came into being.

Lost in the rapture of his celestial trance,
We find our souls joining in this sprightly dance.

Patience

In patience, Sita waits through endless days,
Her heart a captive, longing to be free,
Like lovers lost in traffic's endless maze.

Her mind recalls the tender, loving gaze,
The promise of a home where love should be,
In patience, Sita waits through endless days.

Today we fume when traffic slows our ways,
Impatient hearts, we seek immediacy,
Like lovers lost in traffic's tangled maze.

We curse the moments, caught in modern craze,
Forget the art of waiting, silently,
In patience, Sita waits through endless days.

Her faith unshaken, though the forest sways,
She trusts in love's eventual decree,
Like lovers lost in traffic's tangled maze.

Reflect dear heart, on Sita's calm and steady
grace,
The timeless truth of love's deep constancy,
In patience, Sita waits through endless days,
Like lovers lost in traffic's tangled maze.

Darbari

In the grand old palace, where the moonlight gleams,
Raag Darbari plays, weaving timeless dreams.
Courtyards fill with echoes, ancient and profound,
Each note a whisper, each beat a hallowed sound.

Golden chandeliers cast a gentle, warming light,
Softly illuminating the velvet of the night.
Silk-clad courtiers gather, in reverent array,
Drawn by the magic of the music's sway.

The musicians sit in a circle, poised and still,
Their fingers dance on the strings with practised skill.
The tabla's rhythm pulses like a beating heart,
Each sound a stroke of genius, a master's art.

From the veena's strings, a melody ascends,
As if the heavens and earth it mends.

The sarangi weeps with a voice so pure,
In every note, a longing, in every chord, a cure.

The air is thick with incense, sandalwood and
myrrh.
A fragrance that enchants, as senses start to blur.
Eyes close in rapture, face soft with peace,
As the ragas deep currents offer sweet release.

Peacocks in the garden with their vibrant dance,
The lotus blooms are still, caught in a trance.
Stars seem to twinkle brighter in the velvet sky,
Touched by the music, they shimmer and they
sigh.

In the throne room, the Maharaja sits enthralled,
His regal mask slips, by the music called.
Beside him, the Maharani's eyes are bright,
Lost in the waves of the divine, sacred light.

Maids pause in doorways, captivated too,
Caught in splendour, as each note rings true.
The palace breathes as one, in harmony so
sweet,
Unified by the rhythm, of music's heartbeat.

Time itself seems to pause, held by the sound,
In Raag Darbari's grace, eternity is found.
Hearts swell with ecstasy, minds gently float,

On the divine energy, each transcendent note.

As the final note fades, a hush fills the space,
A moment of pure stillness, a sacred embrace.
Then the applause erupts, a thunderous praise,
For the divine journey, for the emotions to blaze.

In the grand old palace, where dreams were
spun,
Raag Darbari's magic leaves no heart undone.
Its echoes linger, like whispers in the breeze,
A timeless testament to the divine music's power
to please.

Meera

In Meera's heart, devotional fire burned bright,
A love so pure, it soared on the heaven's breeze,
Her soul's deep longing, boundless as the night.

Her days were filled with hymns and songs of
the light,
Each verse a plea, her spirit to appease,
In Meera's heart, devotional fire burned bright.

Through palace halls, her voice would take its
flight,
A melody of love that sought to please,
Her soul's deep longing, boundless as the night.

To the creator's name, she gave her boundless
might,
In every prayer, her heart found sweet release,
In Meera's heart, devotional fire burned bright.

The world around her seemed to fade from sight,
In ecstasy, her mind was set at ease,
Her soul's deep longing, boundless as the night.

Though trials came, her faith was her true light,
Her path to love, no earthly force could seize,
In Meera's heart, devotional fire burned bright,
Her soul's deep longing, boundless as the night.

Birbal the Wise

In a kingdom vast with tales untold,
Lived a man of wisdom, sharp and bold.
His name, like whispers through the air,
Echoes of Birbal, wise and fair.

He sat in court, where questions spun,
With riddles, games, he'd never shun.
In every jest, a lesson hid,
In every tale, a truth he bid.

Oh, wily wit of boundless scope,
A beacon bright for those who hope.
He'd find the way where none could see,
With wisdom's light, he'd set minds free.

Through jest and jape, he'd lead the way,
In laughter's cloak, the truth would stay.
A master of the cunning jest,
In Akbar's Court, he was the best.

When asked which day is best, he'd say,
"Tomorrow's light or yesterday."
A riddles charm in answers clear,
Yet wisdom's heart, it's ever near.

In every word, a puzzle placed,
In every jest, a wisdom traced.
His tales still weave through time and space,
A testament to wits embrace.

So, if you seek a mind that's keen
With answers hidden, yet unseen,
Look to the tales of Birbal the Wise,
Where riddles bloom and truths arise.

The race of life

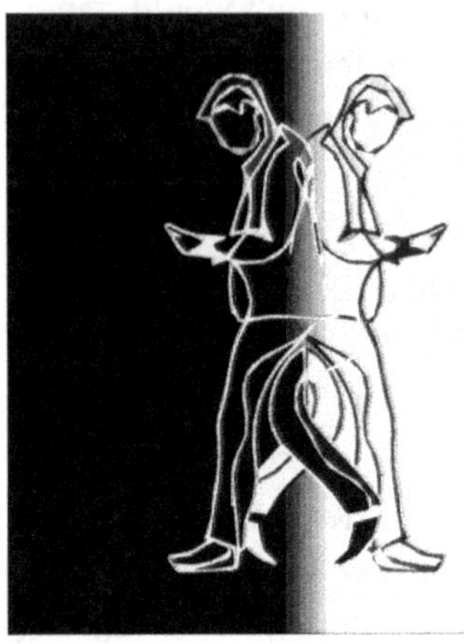

In the bustling streets where neon lights blaze,
Amidst the daily clamour, do traditional values
still rise?
In the whirlwind of progress, do we pause to
admire,
The wisdom of ancestors, that flickers like fire?

Does the rhythm of city life drown out the old
song,
Of unity, respect, where do these belong?
In the race for success, do we leave behind,
The teachings of elders, so gentle, so kind?

In the quest for wealth, do we forget to share,
The blessings bestowed; do we still care?

As skyscrapers rise, do hearts grow tall,
Or does greed consume, leaving nothing at all?

Amidst technology's embrace, do we lose sight,
Of simplicity, humility, in the quest for might?
In the age of information, do we find wisdom's
gate,
Or drown in the noise, left to fate?

In the pursuit of individual dreams, do we
forsake,
The bonds of community, for our own sake?
As the world spins faster, do we hold tight,
To the threads of tradition, in the darkest night?

Do we honour our heritage, or cast it away,
In the glare of modernity's bright display?
In the clash of cultures, do we find harmony,
Or are we torn apart by discord's cacophony?

As we navigate the currents in times relentless
flow,
Do we cherish the past, or let it go?
In the tapestry of modern life, do we weave,
The threads of tradition, or do we deceive?

The questions linger, in the depths of the soul,
As we strive for progress, towards an unknown
goal.

In the clash of old and new, what path shall we choose,
To honour our roots, or simply let it loose?

Oh Weaver!

In the heart of Banaras, where the Ganges flows,
A weaver sits, with hands that know,
The ancient art of silk, in colours bright,
In the gentle glow of the moon's soft light.

Oh weaver, with your nimble fingers so deft,
In the rhythm of your loom, secrets are left,
In the threads you weave, a tale begins to unfold.
Of tradition and beauty, forever untold.

Beneath the starry sky, by the river's edge,
He spins his magic on the ancient pledge,
To craft a saree, so fine and rare,
A masterpiece of silk, beyond compare.

Oh weaver, with your skilful hands,
Creating beauty in distant lands,
In each intricate pattern, stories are spun.
Of love, of life, beneath the sun.

As the Ganges whispers secrets old,
The loom sings a melody, rich and bold,
A symphony of colours, in every thread,
Woven with care, like prayers unsaid.

Oh weaver, with your timeless art,
You capture the essence of a culture's heart,
In the shimmering silk, dreams take flight,
In the dance of the loom, through the night.

Beneath the moon's soft glow, and the river's
gentle flow,
The saree comes alive, with a beauty that's
aglow,
In the heart of Banaras, where traditions
intertwine,
A weaver's craft endures, like a sacred shrine.

Oh weaver, with your hand of gold,
In the tapestry of life, your stories unfold.
With each delicate thread, a legacy is born,
In the beauty of a saree, forever worn.

Life is but a Dream

In the realm of whimsy, where Alice roams,
In wonderland's depths, where fantasy looms,
Caroll spoke of a curious theme,
That life is but a dream, or so it may seem.

Through the looking glass, where reality bends,
Where logic and reason meet playful ends,
Yet in this tale of wonder and gleam,
Lies a whisper of truth, like a distant beam.

For in the land of ancient lore,
Where tales of Gods and demons soar,
Indian wisdom speaks of Maya's sway,
Where illusions dance, night and day.

Moksha, they seek, the souls release,
From Maya's grip, a path to peace,
Through lifetimes of Karma, they strive and
yearn,
For liberation, from Maya's churn.

In Carroll's, dream, and in Indian lore,
Echoes of truth, forevermore,
Life's illusions, its joys and strife,
Melt away on the journey to eternal life.

So, embrace the dream, the dance, the play,
For in its midst, lies truths bright ray,
Life is but a dream, a passing gleam,
Yet in its depths lies Moksha's stream.

Maa (Mother)

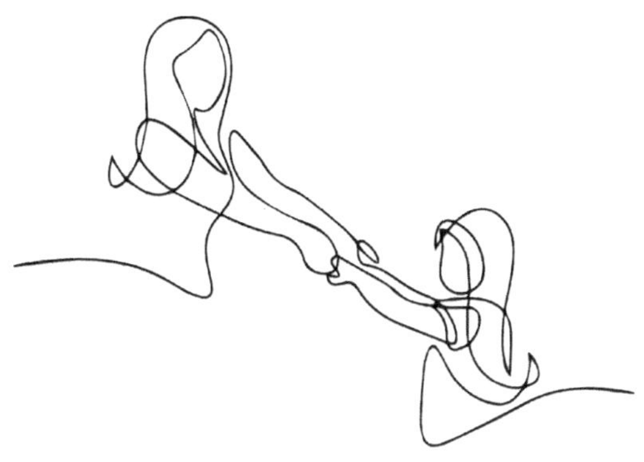

In your embrace, a sanctuary I find,
Maa, your love, forever kind.

In your eyes, stars of guidance shine bright,
Guiding me through life's darkest night.

Your gentle touch, a soothing balm,
In your arms, I find eternal calm.

Through laughter and tears, you're always
nearby,
Maa, your love, forever sincere.

With each heartbeat, your name I adore,
In your love, I find my forevermore.

Grateful I am, for your nurturing grace,
In your love, I find my sacred space.

120

When Love & Hate Collide

In a tumultuous heart, a story unfolds,
Of loves tender embrace, and hates bitter cold.
From the depths of affection to the heights of
disdain,
A journey of emotions, like the sun and rain.

Once upon a time, a world torn apart,
Love's gentle whispers soothed every heart.
In the warmth of a lover's kiss,
Healing began, in moments of bliss.

But shadows lurked in the corners of the soul,
As hate's venomous whispers took their toll.
Jealousy, anger, resentment grew,
Tearing apart what love once knew.

Yet amidst the chaos, a beacon did shine,
A love divine, transcending all time.
In the depths of the soul, a sacred flame,
Ignited by grace, no hate could tame.

For in the arms of the divine, all find solace,
In love's embrace, there is no need to polish.
Forgiveness flows like a gentle stream,
Washing away hate's toxic gleam.

In today's world, where hate runs deep,
Love's power still holds the key to keep.
Through kindness, compassion, and empathy's
gaze,
Healing begins in the most unlikely of ways.

So let love be our guide, in this world so torn,
From hate to love, let us make the turn,
For in love's embrace, and touch divine,
Healing begins, one heart at a time.

Grandmother

My grandmother's eyes, did reflect the moon's
gentle glow,
A divine Goddess in human form, her grace did
flow.

With hands that soothed like a gentle breeze,
She embodied purity, her essence a sacred seed.

In her laughter, echoed the songs of a river's
flow,
A Goddess of Joy, in her presence, my heart did
glow.

Her wisdom, a beacon, like the sun's radiant
light,
Guiding me through the darkness, with her
insight so bright.

With every step she took, the earth lifted her
with delight,
A Goddess of strength, in her presence, all fears
fled without a sight.

Her love, so divine, sweet and pure,
Enveloping me in the warmth, always secure.

In her presence and touch, the family found
solace and peace,
My grandmother, a goddess, her love will never
cease.

I bow before you my grandma, with reverence
and awe,
Gone but not forgotten, a divine Goddess in you
I saw.

The Joy of Life

Under the embrace of vast blue skies, a gentle breeze blows,
The simple pleasures in life, like a fragrant rose.

With each dawn's kiss, the world anew,
The simple pleasures in life, like the morning dew.

A walk in the park, under the sun's warm embrace,
The simple pleasures in life can be found in nature's grace.

A shared meal with your loved ones, laughter in
the air,
The simple pleasures in life can be found with
those who care.

A quiet moment alone, with a good book in
hand,
The simple pleasures in life, found while your
thoughts expand.

A melody that soothes, a songbird's sweet
refrain,
The simple pleasures in life, found in music's
domain.

A tight embrace, a tender touch,
The simple pleasures in life, that mean so much.

A starry night, a sky full of dreams,
The simple pleasures in life, under moonlit
beams.

A heartfelt conversation, with a friend so dear,
The simple pleasures in life can be found in
words sincere.

A cup of tea, shared in good company,
The simple pleasures in life, in camaraderie.

In life's simple moments, true treasures lie,
The simple pleasures in life for all, under the
same sky.

The Artist's Stroke

In hues, the canvas comes to life,
Each stroke a whisper, a testament to the strife.
As the artist's hand dances in sweet embrace,
Love on the canvas unfurls, with beauty and
grace,
Brushes of passion caress the blank expanse,
Crafting a masterpiece, in hues that dance.

With delicate strokes, the artist creates magic,
A tapestry of dreams, both sweet and tragic,
Each brushstroke a dance on the canvas expanse,
In the language of colours, they mix in a trance,

As the painting blossoms, its beauty comes
alive,
In a symphony of love, the colours begin to jive.

The palette sings with joy, in tender embrace,
As the artist's vision emerges, with timeless
grace,
Each stroke a testament, as the painting takes
form,
In a crescendo of colour, where all is soft and
warm,
With each whisper of pigment, the canvas comes
to life,
In the language of art, a story of love and strife..

With every stroke, the artist's story does unfold,
Of an eternal waltz, a story never before told.
As the painting breathes life, through strokes so
bold,
A story of passion, a scene to behold
In a ballet of beauty, the hues align,
To create a memory, immortal in time.

Through the artists hands, a truth is revealed,
A story that till now lay sealed.
The tale of the artist, a masterpiece to keep.

Thinking Out Loud

Is the moon not the mirror of our dreams and
desires intertwined?
Do stars not weave stories in the fabric of our
fate conjoined?

When the river meets the ocean, do they not
whisper secrets old?
Are we not tributaries, merging with love's
infinite hold?

In the silence of the night, do hearts not beat in a
shared rhyme?
Are we not bound by invisible threads, across
distance and time?

When a tree falls in a forest, do we not feel the
earth's soft sigh?
Is our sorrow not a symphony, shared beneath
the same sky?

Do the winds not carry echoes of voices lost and
found?
Are we not the echoes, resonating with a
timeless sound?

When petals unfurl to the sun, do we not bloom
in unity?
Is life not a dance of shadows and light, in sweet
continuity?

In the laughter of a child, do we not hear the
future's call?
Are we not reflections, standing in wonder, after
all?

Is the pain of one not a whisper in the heart of
another, near or far?
Are we not each other's keepers, under the same
celestial star?

When the dawn breaks anew, does it not promise
hope for every soul?
Are we not bound in this eternal weave, each
part of a greater whole?

The Coonoor Club

In Coonoor's cradle, tucked away,

Where misty mornings greet the day,

The toast is crisp, the chicken's gold,

A savoury tale that never gets old.

Feathers fly where rackets swing,

In badminton's rhythmic spring,

But in the air, not just the shuttle,

Friendships form in every scuttle.

Tennis nets amd cricket stumps,

Echoes of cheer and heartbeats thump,

Yet in each match, the scores a jest,

For bonds are what we treasure best.

As twilight falls, the chatter grows,

Of bisons bold and bears that roam,

Stories spun with laughters weave,

From Coonoor's warmth, no soul shall leave.

With wafers in hand and scotch in glass,

We toast to moments that shall pass,

The company is wise and kind

The memories linger on, in heart and mind

At the club, where all is laughter and fun,

And games are played till day is done,

The chicken on toast is just the start,

But it's the company that steals the heart.

Penned

In your hand, I dance with ink and grace,
You pour your heart out through every line you write,
For love's sweet sake, our union finds its place.

Your gentle touch, my nib does softly trace,
A love letter to set your partner's heart alight,
In your hand, I dance with ink and grace.

Upon the page, your words in tender chase,
Crafting whispers meant for a moonlit night,
For love's sweet sake, our union finds its place.

With every stroke, emotions we embrace,
Transforming thoughts into a pure delight,
In your hand, I dance with ink and grace.

Through flowing lines, our shared, secret space,
A tale of love that feels so true and right,
For love's sweet sake, our union finds its place.

Our bond, time can't erase,
Pen and heart truly unite,
In your hand, I dance with ink and grace,
For love's sweet sake, our union finds its place.

Sparring Gloves

In a dim-lit room, they hang with quiet pride,
Once vibrant red, now dulled by time and dust,
These gloves, now still, with tales of battles
fought,
Echoes of cheer and grunts in distant air,
The sparring matches where they found their
worth,
A legacy of strength they can't let fade.

Each worn-out seam and leather's subtle fade,
Speaks volumes of the journey, battles fought,
Of victories claimed, of moments filled with
pride,
These gloves that now, untouched, collect dust,
Silent they lie, yet filled with memories worth,
Still whispering to the silent, sombre sir.

Once they flew swiftly through heated air,
With punches sharp, they made their presence
fade,
They earned their marks, each tear, each scar,
their worth,
Against opponents, fierce encounters fought,
Now time has claimed them, left to gather dust,
Yet in their stillness, they retain their pride.

In countless rings, they've felt the rising pride,
Of wins that sent elation through the air,
Now at rest and covered in dust
Their vibrant colour dimmed by times fade,
Memories linger of the battles fought,
In the silence, echoes hold their worth.

Each punch they landed spoke of their true
worth,
A testament to sweat and effort's pride,
They bore the weight of every match
well-fought,
Now all that moves around them is the air,
The cheers have ceased, the roars of the crowds
now fade,
Yet still they stand, beneath a veil of dust.

Red everlast gloves, now draped in idle dust,
Who once knew glory, proved their mettle's
worth,
Their story etched in leather, though colours
fade,
They stand as a symbol of a fighter's pride,
Of battles won, that linger in the air,
Of every round, and every foe they fought.

Though covered now in dust, their pride won't
fade,
Their worth remains, as battles they once fought,

Hang in the air, where they, in silence, bide.

138

Oh Sun, Shine bright!

Oh sun, shine bright, dispel this misty day,
With your golden rays, warm this Jasmine will
stay.

Through this foggy veil, I seek your touch to
play,
Your gentle warmth, in your embrace I sway.

In the garden's hush, my petals cold and white
Yearn for the golden light and your warmth, a
relieving sight.

With fragrant blooms, I call to you, dear Sun,
To embrace this garden and let me indulge in
some warm fun.

In your bright glow, my essence will come alive,
Your presence turns my grey to a vibrant sunny
jive.

Oh sun, shine bright, I await your grace,
For I yearn to have the sun on my face.

Moth to a Flame

In the depths of night, we yearn, like a moth to a
flame,
Seeking light in shadows, we burn, like a moth
to a flame.

Desires whisper secrets, hearts caught in a glow,
Bound by passions turn, like a moth to a flame.

Truth eludes the weary, wrapped in dreams so
bright,
In illusions, we discern, like a moth to a flame.

Love's tender lure, a beacon in the dark,
In its warmth, we churn, like a moth to a flame.

Folly's path we tread, knowing well the cost,
To wisdom we adjourn, like a month to a flame.

In the dance of fate, we find our place,
Destiny's wheel we spurn, like a moth to a
flame.

Dear life, pour the wine, let the spirit soar,
In your embrace, we yearn, like a moth to a
flame.